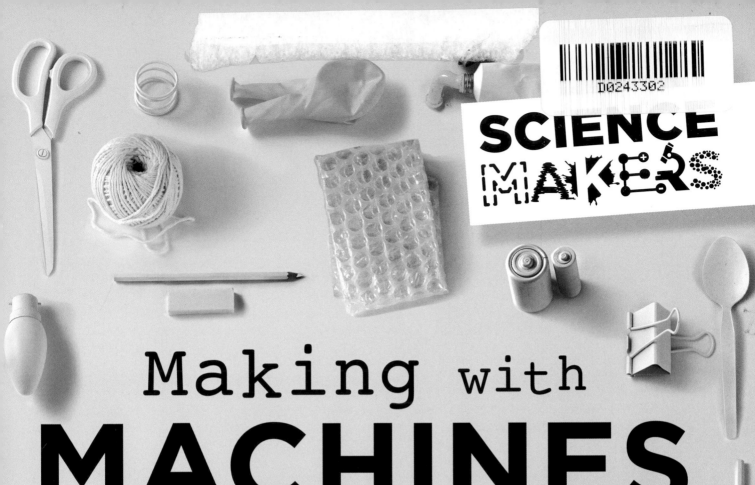

SCIENCE MAKERS

Making with
MACHINES

Anna Claybourne

BUILD **AMAZING PROJECTS** WITH **INSPIRATIONAL SCIENTISTS,** A**ND** ENGINEERS

Published in paperback in Great Britain in 2020 by Wayland
Copyright © Hodder and Stoughton, 2018
All rights reserved.

Editor: Sarah Silver
Designer: Eoin Norton
Picture researcher: Diana Morris

ISBN 978 1 5263 0551 0

Printed in Dubai

Wayland, an imprint of
Hachette Children's Group
Part of Hodder and Stoughton
Carmelite House
50 Victoria Embankment
London EC4Y 0DZ

An Hachette UK Company
www.hachette.co.uk
www.hachettechildrens.co.uk

Note:
In preparation of this book, all due care has been exercised with regard to the instructions, activities and
techniques depicted. The publishers regret that they can accept no liability for any loss or injury sustained.

The website addresses (URLs) included in this book were valid at the time of going to press.
However, because of the nature of the Internet, it is possible that some addresses may have
changed, or sites may have changed or closed down since publication. While the author
and publishers regret any inconvenience this may cause to the readers, no responsibility
for any such changes can be accepted by either the author or the publishers.

CONTENTS

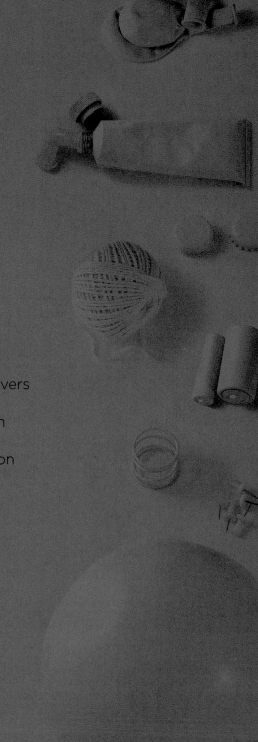

TAKE CARE!

These projects can be made with everyday objects, materials and tools that you can find at home, or in a supermarket, hobby store or DIY store. However, some do involve working with things that are sharp or breakable, or need extra strength to operate. Make sure you have an adult on hand to supervise and to help with anything that could be dangerous, and get permission before you try out any of the projects.

HOW MACHINES WORK

Since ancient times, we've been making our lives easier with the help of machines. From waterwheels and bows and arrows to bicycles, dishwashers and computer technology, human history is full of them. And we all use machines every day, from a simple pair of scissors or a can opener, to cars, phones and satellites.

A robotic arm on the International Space Station can be used to pull supply space craft onboard.

WHAT IS A MACHINE?

A machine is a device that helps us to use forces and motion to do a task. It doesn't have to be something with lots of moving parts. Many basic tools are simple machines. For example, a pair of scissors turns the squeezing force of your hand into a more focused pressure that can cut cleanly through paper or cloth.

Of course, many machines do have lots of moving parts – such as the complex sets of gears inside a clock, or the parts that make up a helicopter, car or robot.

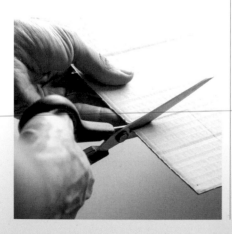

HOW IT WORKS

Machines work by controlling and directing forces. One example is a lever, a simple machine that's an important part of many tools and larger machines. A lever is a rigid bar with a pivot point or fulcrum, which it rotates around.

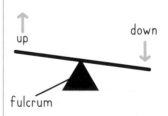

up   down

fulcrum

When you press down on one end of this lever, the other end moves up. A seesaw is a simple lever.

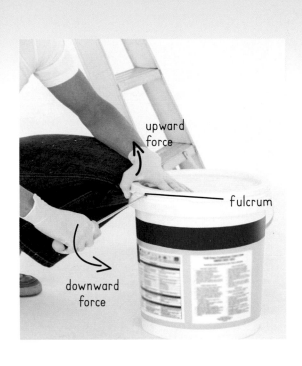

upward force

fulcrum

downward force

LEVER POWER

If the fulcrum is closer to one end, the short end will move a shorter distance than the long end, but will have more pushing power. That's what's happening when you use a spoon or screwdriver to lever the lid off a tin.

fulcrum

A pair of scissors is made up of two levers, connected at the fulcrum.

INVENTING MACHINES

Many of the most important inventions of all time have been machines that people invented to solve problems and achieve new things. The wheel, the propeller, the printing press, the car engine, the telephone, computer technology and aircraft are just a few of them. And we're still coming up with more new machines all the time.

A solar-powered car in a special race for solar-powered vehicles and bicycles.

MACHINE ART

Like everyone else, artists have always used machines to achieve their aims, using scissors, chisels, chainsaws, spray cans, and in recent times, computers to make art. Machines themselves can be artworks too, and many modern artists make moving machine sculptures, automated drawing machines that make their own pictures, or machines that create an atmosphere with light and sound. Meanwhile, making your own DIY machines at home is a big part of the popular crafting and making trend.

The *Bucket Fountain*, in Wellington, New Zealand, is a moving sculpture powered by water, designed by Burren and Keen.

THING FLINGER

Make a working battle catapult inspired by Archimedes, one of the greatest machine-makers of all time.

A later illustration showing how one of Archimedes' catapults worked.

MAKER PROFILE:

Archimedes
(c. 287–212 BCE)

Archimedes was an ancient Greek from Syracuse, a Greek settlement in Sicily. A great mathematician, scientist and engineer, he designed ships and invented useful machines, such as the Archimedes screw for pumping water. When the Romans attacked Syracuse, the city asked Archimedes to help defend it. He came up with several brilliant weapons, including a claw for overturning enemy ships, and powerful new catapult designs.

Eureka! (I've got it!)
- Attributed to Archimedes after he found the solution to a science problem.

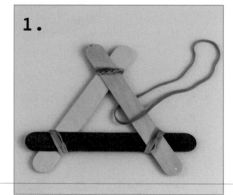

1.

WHAT YOU NEED

- lolly sticks or craft sticks
- assorted elastic bands
- small wooden or plastic spoon
- a craft knife or scissors
- a small craft foam or cotton wool ball

Step 1.

Use three sticks to make a triangle by wrapping elastic bands around the ends. Before joining up the last corner, thread a strong elastic band onto the triangle.

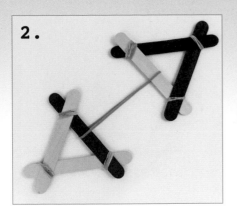

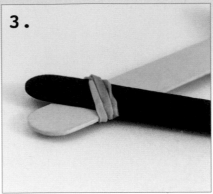

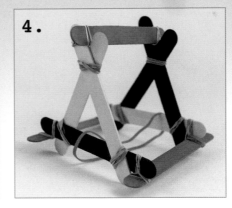

Step 2.
Make another triangle the same way, with the other end of the strong elastic band threaded onto it.

Step 3.
Roll the elastic bands at the corners down the sticks, so that the ends poke out more.

Step 4.
Use more elastic bands to attach a stick between each of the two triangles at the corners. You should now have a frame made of sticks. Stand it up so that the loose elastic band reaches across the bottom of the frame.

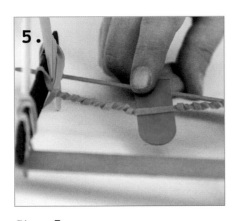

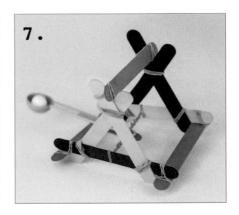

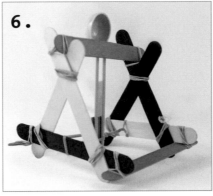

Step 5.
Ask an adult to cut a short length of craft stick using a craft knife or scissors. Put it inside the loose elastic band, and twist it until the band is tightly twisted up.

Step 6.
Push the handle of the spoon into the twisted elastic band, on top of the piece of stick, so that it rests against the bar that runs across the top of the frame.

Step 7.
Holding the frame steady, pull the spoon down, then let it go. It should spring back up. Do this again, with a foam or cotton wool ball in the spoon. Ready, aim, fire!

STORING UP ENERGY

When you wind up the elastic band, the energy you use to twist the elastic gets stored in it. When you let go of the spoon, the stored energy is suddenly released, and flings the spoon around in a circle. The bar at the top stops the spoon, and the ball then keeps going and flies through the air. Instead of elastic rubber, the ancient Greeks used rope made from stretchy animal sinews – body parts that attach muscles to bones.

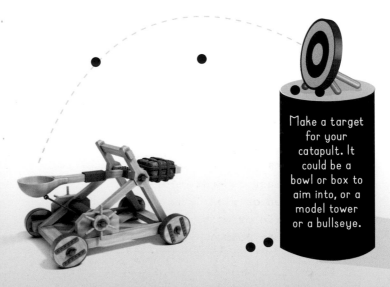

Make a target for your catapult. It could be a bowl or box to aim into, or a model tower or a bullseye.

CABLE DELIVERY

Build your own indoor cable car to deliver messages, toys or snacks to their destination.

MAKER PROFILE:

Adam Wybe
(1584–1653)

Dutch engineer and inventor Adam Wybe was well-known for designing all kinds of useful things – windmills, water wheels, bridges, and a fire-fighting water pump. His most famous creation, in 1644, was his aerial tramway, an early version of the cable car. Wybe's invention didn't carry people, but buckets of soil for building a city wall. It had a long loop of cable with over 100 buckets attached, which circulated around a set of pulleys on wooden towers.

WHAT YOU NEED

- two plastic pulley wheels (from a hobby or hardware store, or online)
- long cocktail sticks or wooden skewers
- four craft sticks or wide lolly sticks

- a hole punch
- erasers or small corks
- strong string
- scissors
- a small cardboard box
- a marker pen to decorate

An illustration of Adam Wybe's 1644 aerial tramway in Gdansk, Poland.

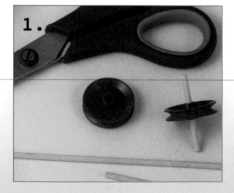

Step 1.

Ask an adult to cut two 4-cm lengths of cocktail stick or skewer, using the scissors or craft knife. Push them through the centre of each pulley wheel.

> Instead of real pulley wheels, you can use the middle part of a medium or large Lego wheel, with the tyre removed.

Step 2.
Use the hole punch to carefully make holes in both ends of each craft or lolly stick. Put one stick on each side of the pulley wheels.

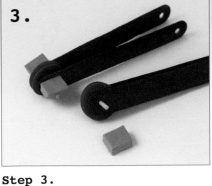

Step 3.
Cut the erasers or corks if necessary and push them onto the ends of the sticks, to hold everything in place. Make sure the wheels can turn freely.

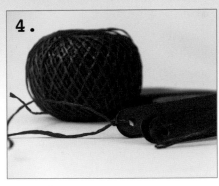

Step 4.
Cut two 30-cm lengths of string and use them to tie the other ends of the craft sticks together, leaving the long ends free.

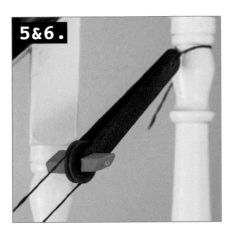

Step 5.
With an adult to help, find two safe, firm anchor points, one high and one low – such as bannisters, coat hooks or window locks or handles. Or ask an adult to put a nail or screw hook into a door frame or skirting board.

Step 6.
Tie your two pulleys to the anchor points. Then thread a long piece of string through both pulleys and tie it tightly to make a taut loop.

Step 7.
Use the cardboard box to make a cable car with triangular points on the side pieces. Punch holes in the tops of the triangles and tie a loop of string through them.

Step 8.
Tie the cable car to the pulley cable, just above where you knotted it. You can now pull the pulley cable at one end to make the cable car travel up and down.

SMOOTH MOVEMENT

A pulley wheel is a simple machine that allows a string or cable to move past a fixed point smoothly, without rubbing and wearing away. It's a useful part of many machines, especially cable cars. Today, there are passenger-carrying cable cars all over the world that work like Adam Wybe's.

POWERED FLIGHT

Copy the Wright brothers and make a real propeller-powered plane.

MAKER PROFILE:

Wilbur Wright
(1867–1912)
Orville Wright
(1871–1948)

Orville and Wilbur Wright were American brothers who are famous for making the first controlled, powered flight in a heavier-than-air machine. They spent several years studying and designing wings, gliders and propellers, before developing their famous flying machine, the *Wright Flyer*. On 17 December 1903, near Kitty Hawk, North Carolina, USA, the *Wright Flyer* made its first proper flight, over a distance of about 40 m, with Orville on board. (Wilbur got the next turn!)

The desire to fly is an idea handed down to us by our ancestors.
- Wilbur Wright

WHAT YOU NEED

- a pencil
- stiff card
- thin card
- scissors
- a metal paper clip
- sticky tape
- a thin drinking straw
- an extra-wide straw
- old felt-tip pen with a wide, cylindrical plastic lid
- a bradawl or large, sharp needle
- pliers
- a long, thin elastic band
- a wooden skewer

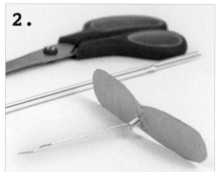

Step 1.
Draw a propeller on the stiff card and cut it out. Twist it gently to angle the propeller blades in different directions. Straighten out the paper clip and push it through the middle of the propeller. Bend 1 cm of the clip over at the end, and tape it firmly against the propeller to hold it in place.

Step 2.
Cut a 0.5 cm length of drinking straw. Thread it on to the paper clip.

3.

Step 3.

Remove the felt-tip pen lid, and ask an adult to make a hole through the top of it, in the middle, using the bradawl or needle. Push the paper clip through the hole from the top. It should be able to turn around freely. (If it doesn't, make the hole bigger.)

4.

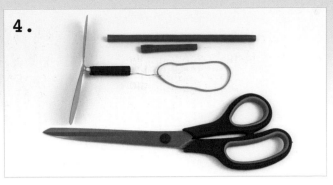

Step 4.

Use the pliers to bend the straight end of the paper clip over to make a hook. Loop the elastic band into the hook. If the wider straw has a bendy part, cut this end off now.

5.

Step 5.

Use the wooden skewer to push the other end of the elastic band down inside the straw, and out at the other end. Cut a 1-cm piece of the thin straw and push it through the end of the elastic band, to hold it in place.

6.

Step 6.

Now fit the pen lid over the end of the straw. If it doesn't fit over the straw, line the lid and the straw up neatly and tape around them to hold them together.

7.

Step 7.

Cut a wing shape, a tail fin and a tail wing from the thinner card. Tape them to the straw, keeping clear of the propeller. Trim them to fit if they are too big.

8.

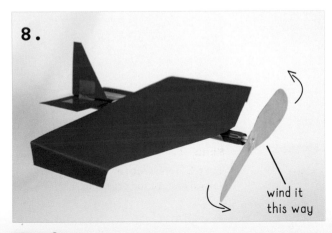

wind it this way

Step 8.

To make the plane work, twist the propeller until the elastic band is tightly wound, then let the plane go. It will only work if you twist the propeller in the right direction!

HOW PROPELLERS WORK

As a propeller turns, it slices through the air, and its angled blades push air backwards. This in turn pushes the propeller (and the plane) forwards. A propeller also needs a source of power to turn it. In your model it's an elastic band, but the Wright brothers used a lightweight petrol engine.

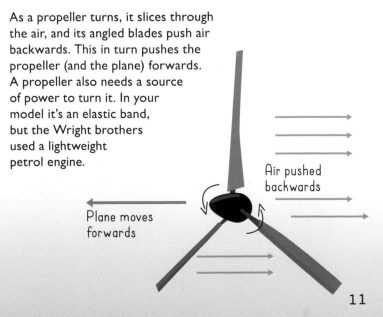

Air pushed backwards

Plane moves forwards

WEATHER MACHINE

Make a barometer to detect air pressure, which can help you to forecast the weather.

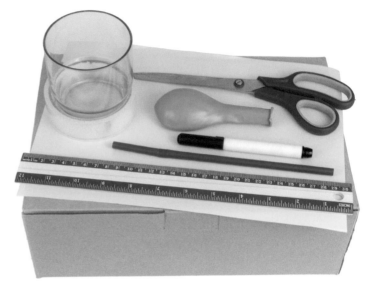

MAKER PROFILE:

Lucien Vidie
(1805–1866)

In 1843, French scientist Lucien Vidie developed a new type of barometer. Barometers, which measure air pressure, had existed for 200 years. But earlier designs used a container of liquid such as water or mercury, making them hard to move around. Vidie's version had a sealed metal box, called an aneroid cell. Changes in air pressure changed the shape of the box, which was linked to a set of levers so that the pressure could be recorded or shown on a dial.

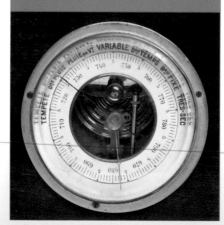

Lucien Vidie's barometer design.

WHAT YOU NEED

- a glass jam jar or tumbler
- a balloon
- scissors
- sticky tape
- a drinking straw
- a shoebox or other similar box
- a ruler
- plain paper
- a pen

1.

Step 1.
Cut the end off the balloon using the scissors. Stretch the rest of the balloon over the top of the jar, making it as flat as possible. Use tape to hold it in place around the sides.

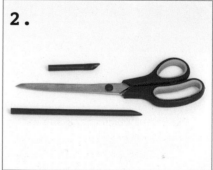

2.

Step 2.
Cut off the tip of the straw at a sharp angle to make a pointer. If the straw is bendy, use the straight end to make the pointer.

Step 3.

Press the other end of the straw flat, and use a small piece of tape to attach it to the middle of the balloon skin.

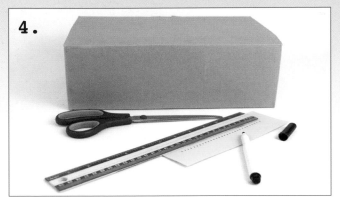

Step 4.

Cut a piece of paper that will fit onto the side of the box. Working up from the bottom of the paper, use the ruler and pen to mark a dot every 0.5 cm.

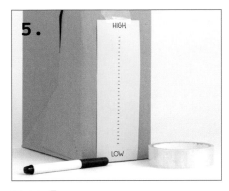

Step 5.

Draw a line at the level of each dot to make a scale. Write 'High' at the top of the scale and 'Low' at the bottom. Tape the paper onto the box.

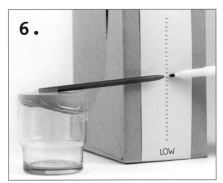

Step 6.

Stand the glass next to the box, so that the straw points to the scale. Mark a dot to show the level of the straw.

Step 7.

Leave the barometer where it won't change temperature much (as this will affect the reading). Check it at the same time each day to see if it shows higher or lower pressure.

Low pressure is more likely to cause rain and wind. High pressure usually means calmer, sunnier weather.

AIR UP, AIR DOWN

Air pressure is caused by the weight of the air around the Earth, which changes in each place as air moves around. When the air pressure is high, air is piling up and sinking, and presses down on the balloon skin. When pressure is low, the balloon skin rises again. The straw is a simple lever – when the balloon skin moves up or down, the other end of the straw moves the opposite way.

WHAT'S IT GOT TO DO WITH THE WEATHER?

When air pressure is low, surrounding air rushes and swirls inwards, causing wind. It then gets pushed upwards and gets cooler, leading to clouds and rain. High pressure makes air sink and spread out, so it's calmer and less cloudy.

BUBBLES GALORE

Build your own bubble machine to fill the air with bubbles!

WHAT YOU NEED

- 8 or more small bottles of bubbles with plastic blowers
- an old, unwanted CD
- a wide plastic tub, such as an ice cream tub
- a wooden spoon with a straight handle
- extra large wire paper clips, or stiff garden wire and wire cutters
- duct tape or other strong tape
- scissors
- a battery-powered mini fan
- extra bubble mixture

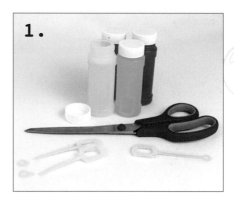

1.

Step 1.
Take all the blowers out of the bubble bottles, rinse them clean and dry them well. Use scissors to snip off their handles, leaving the stems on.

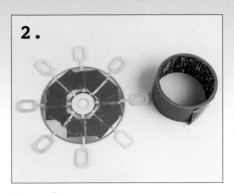

Step 2.

Use strong tape to attach the bubble blowers to the printed side of the CD, so that they stick out all around the edge.

Step 3.

Fit the spoon handle into the hole in the CD. It will probably be loose, so wrap duct tape around the middle of the handle until it makes a tight fit.

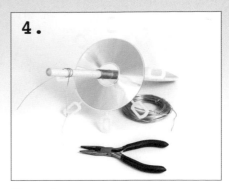

Step 4.

Straighten out a paper clip, or ask an adult to cut a length of garden wire about 20 cm long. Wind the middle section of the wire around the end of the spoon handle, so that it fits loosely.

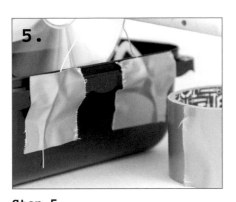

Step 5.

Tape the ends of the wire to the outside of the tub. Do the same with another paper clip or wire at the other end of the spoon handle, and tape it to the other side.

Step 6.

Check that the CD can spin freely in the tub, without any of the bubble blowers hitting the bottom or sides. If they do, move the wires higher up, or switch to a larger tub.

Step 7.

Pour the bubble mixture from your bottles into the tub, and top up with extra mixture until it covers the lowest bubble blower.

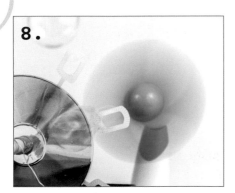

Step 8.

Stand the fan next to the tub, pointing at the blowers. If your fan is too small for this, tape it to the side of the tub instead. Switch the fan on, and turn the spoon handle.

WORKING TOGETHER

This machine makes use of a turning wheel to keep the bubble blowers dipping in and out of the mixture. It also uses a propeller – a fan is a simple propeller that pushes air forwards to make a breeze. A machine that's made up of two or more basic machines working together is called a compound machine.

AT THE TOUCH OF A TOE

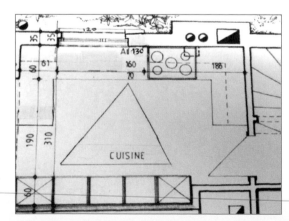

You've probably used a pedal bin, but have you thought about how they work? Find out – and make your own.

MAKER PROFILE:

Lillian Gilbreth
(1878–1972)

American engineer Dr Lillian Gilbreth was an expert in how to work in a faster, more efficient way, to save time and energy. She studied both psychology (the human mind) and engineering, to help her design products and systems to make tasks easier. Gilbreth hated housework, and came up with several inventions to make it less stressful. They included refrigerator door shelves, electric can openers, ergonomic kitchen layouts, and the pedal bin.

WHAT YOU NEED

- a medium-sized cardboard packaging box
- packing tape
- a ruler
- a marker pen or biro
- a craft knife or scissors
- a large wooden spoon
- stiff card
- craft glue
- duct tape
- two wooden rulers or flat spatulas
- patterned paper to decorate

Gilbreth invented the 'work triangle' model of kitchen design, which is still used today.

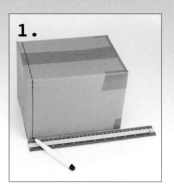

Step 1.

Tape the cardboard box closed with the packing tape. Mark a line around three sides of the box, 1 cm below the top. On the fourth side, draw a dotted line.

Step 2.

Use scissors or a craft knife (with an adult to help) to cut along the three solid lines. Score the dotted line by lightly running the knife or scissors along it.

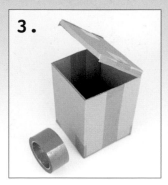

Step 3.

Fold upwards along the dotted line to make a flapping lid. Tape down any loose flaps inside the base or lid.

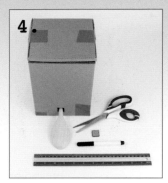

Step 4.

Cut a hole 2 cm x 2 cm in the front of the box, 2 cm above the base. Push the spoon handle into the hole. When you press on the spoon 'pedal', the handle end inside should lift up.

Step 5.

Cut two strips of stiff card, 3-4 cm wide and slightly longer than the height of the box. Cut a notch in the bottom of each strip, the same width as the spoon handle. Glue the two strips together.

Step 6.

Push the double strip down to fit over the end of the spoon handle, inside the box. Trim the top of the strip so that it just touches the inside of the box lid when it's closed.

Step 7.

Use duct tape to attach the top of the strip to the underside of the lid, about 3 cm away from the hinge.

Step 8.

Tape the two rulers underneath the box, one on each side, so that they stick out as far as the spoon pedal. (These stop the bin from tipping forward.) Turn the bin the right way up and test it.

LILLIAN'S LEVERS

The pedal in a pedal bin is a simple lever. When you push one end down, the other end pushes up to lift the lid. The lid itself is a lever too. The upwards movement close to the hinge makes the front of the lid lift up much further.

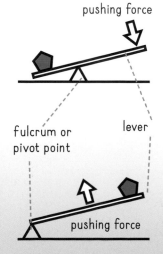

pushing force

fulcrum or pivot point

lever

pushing force

Cover your bin with patterned paper to decorate and use a bin liner to keep your rubbish away from the mechanism.

SNACK MACHINE

Make your own vending machine, based on a two-thousand-year-old design.

MAKER PROFILE:

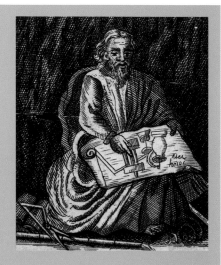

Hero of Alexandria
(CE 10–70)

Ancient inventor Hero of Alexandria was Greek, but lived in Egypt. He was a tireless, endlessly experimenting engineer and inventor who came up with all kinds of machines that we think of as modern ideas, although he lived 2,000 years ago. They included a programmable robot on wheels, an early steam turbine, automatic doors, a mechanical puppet theatre, and the world's first coin-operated vending machine. Hero's vending machine was used in temples to dispense holy water, but a cardboard version that dispenses sweets is a bit less messy.

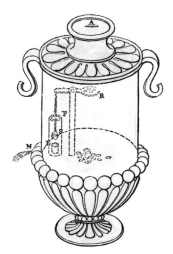

A drawing of Hero of Alexandria's vending machine, showing the working parts inside.

WHAT YOU NEED

- two small, sturdy cardboard packaging boxes
- a larger box with a lid, such as a large shoebox
- sticky tape
- strong packing tape
- scissors
- extra-large wire paper clip, or garden wire and wire cutters
- a drinking straw
- a craft stick or small ruler
- a paper cup
- a small elastic band
- stiff card
- coins
- small sweets

1.

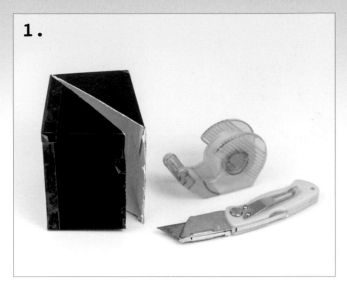

2.

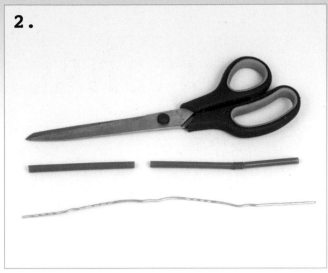

Step 1.

Tape one of the small boxes closed. Then cut across each end diagonally, from one corner to the other. Cut along one edge between the diagonal cuts, so that the box can flap open. This is the dispensing box.

Step 2.

Straighten out the paper clip, or cut a length of garden wire about 20 cm long. Cut a length of drinking straw slightly shorter than the width of the small box, and thread it onto the wire.

3.

4.

5.

Step 3.

Bend the two ends of the wire down, leaving a straight bridge in the middle where the straw is. Tape the ends of the wire to the back of the box, behind the hinge, so that the straight part sticks up above the box.

Step 4.

Cut the base off the paper cup to make a small round tray. Cut off one side to leave a flat edge about 3 cm long. Tape the tray to the end of the stick or ruler, with the edge of the tray facing away from the stick.

Step 5.

Now use tape to attach the middle of the stick or ruler to the top of the straw, with the tray facing away from the box. It should be able to tip to and fro like a seesaw.

6.

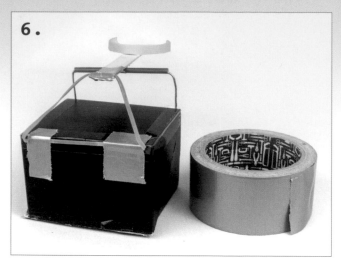

Step 6.

Loop the elastic band over the other end of the stick or ruler, above the box. Use strong tape to fix the elastic band to the box in two places, as shown. When you press down on the tray, the box flap should open slightly.

7.

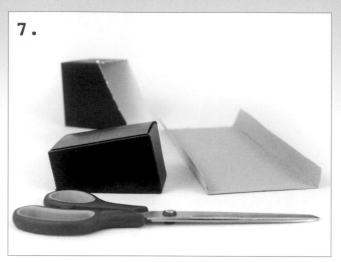

Step 7.

Cut a piece of stiff card about 10 cm wide and 20 cm long. Fold the sides up about 1 cm to make a slide. Take the second small box and cut it off at an angle, making a sloping base for the card slide to rest on.

8&9.

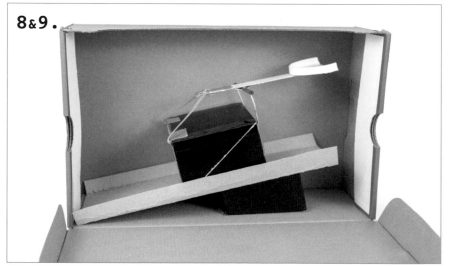

10.

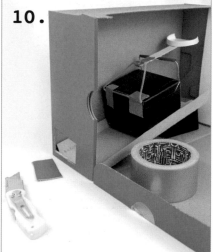

Step 8.

Stand the larger box on its side, and stand the slide on its base inside, so that the bottom of the slide touches the end of the box. Take the dispensing box you have made, and rest this at the top of the slide, facing downwards.

Step 9.

Check everything fits inside the larger box and that the stick can still move freely up and down, making the box lid open and shut. (If not, make the slide shorter or the slide base lower, or switch to a bigger box.)

Step 10.

Once you're happy it all fits, tape the base to the bottom of the outer box, and place the dispensing box on the slide. Cut a hole in the outer box at the bottom of the slide for the sweets to come out of.

11.

Step 11.

Cut a coin slot in the top of the outer box, right above the tray on the end of the stick. Take the dispensing box out and put some sweets inside it, close it, then put it back in position and tape it in place.

TROUBLESHOOTING

- It may take a little tweaking to get everything to work.

- Try adjusting the length of the elastic band if necessary.

- Move the stick further forwards or back where it attaches to the straw.

- If too many sweets come out, or the lid doesn't close properly, tape one or two coins to the top of the dispensing box at the front.

12.

Step 12.

Drop a large coin through the slot. It should hit the tray and lift the front of the box open for a moment, until the coin slides off and the box closes again – releasing a small handful of sweets. If it works, put the outer lid on to hide the mechanism.

fulcrum or pivot point

coin

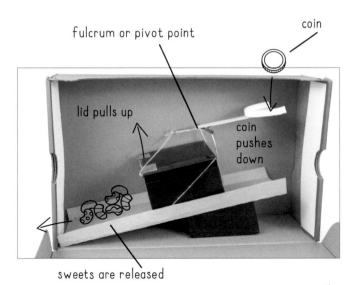

lid pulls up

coin pushes down

sweets are released

A MACHINE FOR EVERYTHING

Hero's idea certainly took off! There are now millions of vending machines all over the world. As well as snacks and drinks, you can get all kinds of other things from vending machines, including live crabs and lobsters, hot pizza, books, fresh lettuce, make-up, and new socks, shoes, pants or tights!

LIFTING LEVER

Although this vending machine is for sweets instead of water, it works exactly the same way as Hero's did. When a coin is dropped in, it pushes down a lever, and the other end of the lever lifts up. It pulls up the lid to let some of the sweets out – until the coin falls off the lever, and it drops back down. In Hero's version, the lever lifted a plug at the bottom of a container of water, letting a little water out, until it came down again.

A food and drinks vending machine.

FLAPPING BIRD

Build your own bird automaton that bobs up and down and flaps its wings.

MAKER PROFILE:

Fi Henshall
(1981–)

Automata are machines that make mechanical movements, often in the form of model people or animals. They date back to ancient times, and are popular as an art form. British sculptor Fi Henshall is a modern artist who makes automata from wood, wire and old tin boxes. Her works often feature flying animals or women, mythical creatures and miniature versions of machines such as bicycles. By turning a handle, the models can be made to move, and sometimes make sounds such as birdsong.

> The range of things that can be achieved merely by the turning of a handle intrigues me.
> - *Fi Henshall*

Fi Henshall's automaton *Secretary Bird*.

WHAT YOU NEED

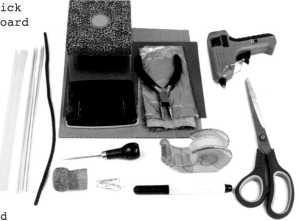

- craft foam or thick corrugated cardboard
- scissors
- a marker pen
- strong glue or a hot glue gun
- a bradawl or thick needle
- wooden skewers
- sticky tape
- a hole punch
- a cork
- strong, stiff card
- four small metal paperclips
- wire cutters
- a pipe cleaner
- three bendy drinking straws
- a small, sturdy cardboard box with a separate lid
- colourful tissue paper or wrapping paper

1.

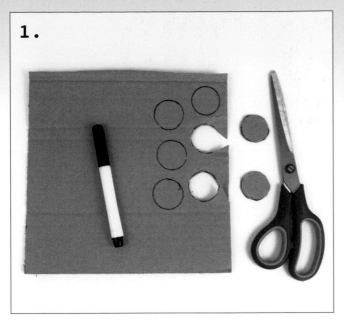

Step 1.
On your craft foam or thick card, draw six circles, each about 3 cm across. (Draw around a circular object to make sure they are all the same.) Carefully cut the circles out, and glue three of them together in a neat stack.

2.

Step 2.
Mark a dot on the top of the stack, between the centre and the edge. Use the bradawl or thick needle to make a hole through all three discs where the dot is. Squirt some glue into the hole.

3.

4.

5.

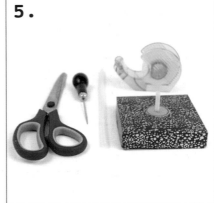

Step 3.
Make two holes in opposites sides of your box, about half way down. Stick a wooden skewer into one side, through the hole in the discs, and out of the other side. Make sure the discs are about half way along the skewer. When you turn the skewer, the discs should bob up and down.

Step 4.
Glue two of the remaining discs together and make a hole through the centre. Stick the blunt end of a wooden skewer into the hole. Then glue the third disc on to the bottom, holding the skewer in place.

Step 5.
Make a hole in the middle of the lid of the box, and use the scissors to make it wider. Cut a piece of drinking straw about 3 cm long and fit it into the hole. Wrap the straw in a layer of sticky tape to make it a tight fit.

6.

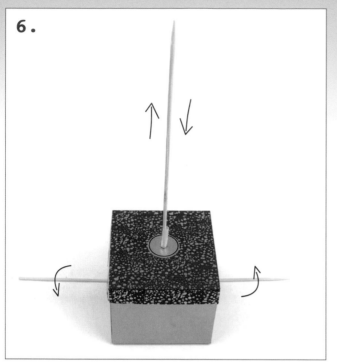

Step 6.

Thread the skewer you made in step 4 up through the straw, so that the end with the disc on it is underneath the lid. Place the lid on to the box. When you turn the horizontal skewer, the vertical one should move up and down, as the discs turn against each other.

7.

Step 7.

Now make your bird. Draw two long, feathered wing shapes on the stiff card, and cut them out. Use the hole punch to cut two holes in the wider end of each wing.

8.

Step 8.

Ask an adult to cut a loop off each paper clip with the wire cutters, to make four small U-shapes. Loop these through the holes in the wings, and push the ends into the sides of the cork. Check the wings can move up and down.

9.

Step 9.

Use the bradawl to make a hole in one end of the cork near the top. Cut a piece of pipe cleaner 4 cm long, and stick one end into the hole. Make a head from a triangle of card folded in half. Glue it onto the pipe cleaner, and draw on eyes.

10.

Step 10.

Cut feather shapes from the tissue or wrapping paper, and glue them to the bird's head and tail. Make a hole in the underside of the cork using the bradawl, and gently push the vertical skewer into it.

11.

12.

13.

Step 11.

Cut the long ends off two drinking straws to make two short bendy sections. Bend them at right angles and tape them to the undersides of the bird's wings, with one part of each straw pointing downwards.

Step 12.

Make two holes in the top of the box using the bradawl, next to the sides. Push two more skewers down into the holes, being careful to avoid the horizontal skewer inside. Cut the tops of the skewers off level with the wings.

Step 13.

Fit the two skewers into the straws under the bird's body, so that they hold the wings steady, but they can still move. Turn the horizontal skewer, and the bird should move up and down and flap its wings.

TWEAK IT

You may need to adjust the parts slightly to make everything work smoothly. Make sure the two discs inside the box are still lined up. If the wings don't move freely, adjust the positions of the straws.

CHANGING MOVEMENTS

The flapping bird machine works using a very important part of machine technology – converting one type of movement into another. The horizontal skewer, called a crankshaft in engineering, moves in a circular or rotary motion. The shape of the disc attached to the crankshaft changes this circular motion into an up-and-down or to-and-fro movement, which engineers call reciprocating motion.

Converting one type of movement to another like this is essential in many types of machines, such as car engines.

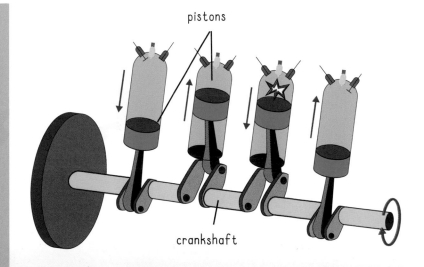

Inside a car, pistons move up and down. This movement turns a crankshaft, which makes the wheels spin around. An up-and down movement turns into a rotating movement – the opposite of how the bird works.

JITTER CRITTER

Make your very own vibrating, jumping and jittering robot creatures.

MAKER PROFILE:

Chico Bicalho
(1960–)

Chico Bicalho is a Brazilian artist, designer and photographer. In the 1990s, he began developing wind-up vibrating mini-robots, known as Critters, which became a popular toy around the world. They move thanks to a vibrating motion that makes them jump, dance and skitter around on their wire legs. Bicalho's Critters are powered by clockwork, but vibration can also be used to make battery-powered robots, often known as vibrobots.

WHAT YOU NEED

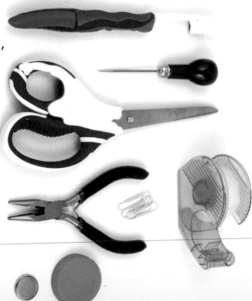

- a vibrating toothbrush, or a mini vibration motor from an electronics store
- a coin battery, such as a watch battery
- pliers
- scissors
- strong sticky tape
- a plastic milk bottle top
- a large needle or bradawl tool
- coloured paper clips

I want to create objects that are both humorous, and unpredictable in behaviour.
— *Chico Bicalho*

1.

Step 1.
Ask an adult to make six holes in opposite sides of the bottle top, using a large needle or bradawl. Straighten out three paper clips and push them through the holes to make the critter legs. Bend the ends over with pliers to make feet.

2.

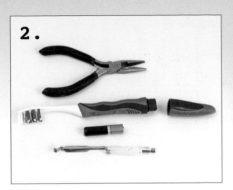

Step 2.

If you are using a toothbrush, ask an adult to take it apart to get the vibration motor out. The motor will be attached to the part that holds the battery, which can be pulled out using pliers.

3.

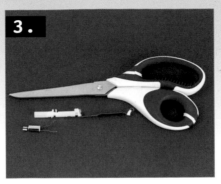

Step 3.

Carefully cut the two wires attached to the motor, leaving them both as long as possible, and pull out the motor. Ask an adult to use scissors to remove some plastic coating from the ends of the wires.

4.

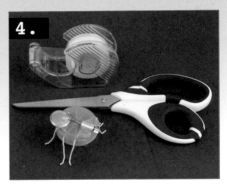

Step 4.

Use a small, narrow sliver of tape to attach the motor to the top of your bottle top critter, on one side. Use another piece of tape to stick the end of the red wire to the underside of the coin battery.

Step 5.

Take another piece of tape and stick it to the end of the blue wire. Press it down onto the top of the battery, and stick the tape down onto the critter to hold both the wires and the battery in place.

MAKING IT SHAKE

A motor makes a spinning motion when electricity runs through it. A vibration motor has an 'offset' weight attached to it – a weight that is heavier on one side. When it spins, this makes the motor, and whatever it's attached to, shake to and fro. Vibration motors are used in toothbrushes, toys and mobile phones (to make them buzz).

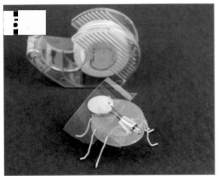

Step 6.

When you press down the blue wire, it should connect the battery to the motor, and make it start spinning. Put the jitter critter down on a flat surface, and let it go!

MORE BOTS

Try attaching your vibration motor to:

• A toothbrush head (ask an adult to cut it off for you)

• A pizza saver or box stand (three-legged plastic stand from a takeaway pizza box)

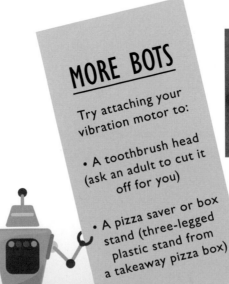

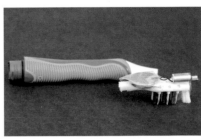

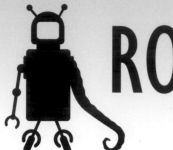

ROBOT TENTACLE

Need to grab something, or tap your friend on the shoulder? Use your tentacle!

MAKER PROFILE:

Kaylene Kau
(1988–)

In 2010, Taiwanese-American industrial design student Kaylene Kau made headlines in the world of design and technology, after designing an artificial arm that worked like an octopus tentacle. Instead of copying the full set of movements of a human arm, she looked at the jobs that people use prosthetic (artificial) arms to do. She developed the tentacle to hold objects while working with another, fully functional arm.

Kaylene Kau's prototype prosthetic tentacle arm is designed to replace the lower half of the human arm. It can grasp objects by curling up like an octopus tentacle.

What futures do we need? ... What worlds do we want to create?
– *Kaylene Kau*

WHAT YOU NEED

- foam pipe insulation tubing (from a DIY or hardware store)
- duct tape or other strong tape
- a marker pen
- a pencil

- a ruler
- scissors
- drinking straws
- strong string
- a metal keyring

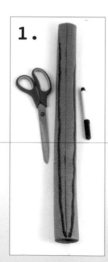

Step 1.
Cut a length of tubing about 50 cm long. Mark a long V-shape along it, starting from a point on one end, and widening to opposite sides of the tube at the other.

2.

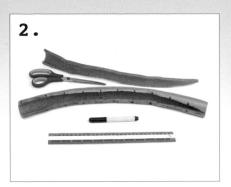

Step 2.

Carefully cut out the V-shape, leaving a piece of tube that is more tube-shaped at one end and narrower towards the other. Mark a dot every 5 cm along it.

3.

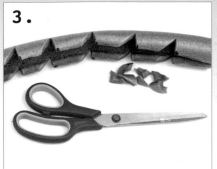

Step 3.

At each dot, cut a smaller 'V'-shape, about 2 cm wide and 2 cm deep, out of the side of the tubing. Do the same along the other side, so that the 'V'-shapes line up.

4.

Step 4.

The tube can now curl up in sections. Count how many sections you have, and cut the same number of short lengths of drinking straw, each about 2 cm long.

5.

Step 5.

Starting at the wider end, push the two sides of the first section together. Cut a small piece of tape and press it onto the inside of the tube to fix the two sides in place.

6.

Step 6.

Put a piece of straw between the two edges, and stick another piece of tape over the top. This will hold the section together strongly, with the straw inside the join.

7.

Step 7.

Do the same for all the other sections. For the smallest sections, use the end of a pencil to press the tape against the join from the inside.

8.

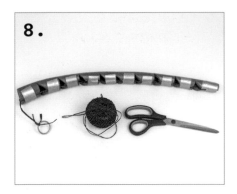

Step 8.

Thread a long piece of string through all the straws. At the smallest section, tie it tightly and secure with a piece of tape. Tie the other end of the string to the keyring.

TUBE CONTROL

When a tube curls over to one side, it gets shorter on that side. A tube or cylinder shape can be controlled by shortening strings along the side, or sides, to make it curl up. Our own fingers work this way, using string-like tendons inside our hands, and so do octopuses' tentacles and elephants' trunks.

To use the tentacle, hold it by the base and pull the keyring to make it curl up.

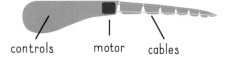

controls   motor   cables

The strings inside Kau's robot tentacle.

GLOSSARY

air pressure The pushing force created by the weight of the air in the atmosphere.

aneroid cell A sealed container with a vacuum inside, used to make a barometer that works without using liquid.

Archimedes screw A pump invented by Archimedes, which uses a turning screw to move water from a lower to a higher level.

automaton A mechanical model that can be made to move, usually by turning a handle.

barometer A device for measuring air pressure.

cable A thick, string rope or cord often used in construction or transport.

compound machine A machine made up of two or more simple machines.

crankshaft A long rod or cylinder that can rotate, found in some types of machine.

energy The power to do work or make things happen.

engineer Someone who designs or builds machines, structures or engines.

engineering The theory and design of machines, engines and structures.

fulcrum The point that a lever pivots or rotates around.

gears Wheels that lock into each other and make each other turn, as a way of transmitting or changing the speed of rotary motion.

glider An aircraft that flies without an engine, using gravity or air currents.

ergonomic Designed to be comfortable to use.

lever A simple machine made up of a rigid bar that turns or pivots around a fixed point.

mechanical Working using a machine or machines.

mercury A silvery-looking metal that is liquid at room temperature.

motion Another word for movement, often used by scientists and engineers.

piston A cylinder or disc that moves to and fro inside a tube, found in some types of machines.

propeller A device made of two or more angled blades, that rotates to push against a fluid such as water or air.

prosthetic An artificial or replacement body part.

prototype An early working model or first version of an invention.

psychology The study of the human mind and personality.

pulley A wheel with a cord or cable that moves around it, used to pull or lift an object.

reciprocating motion A repeating up-and-down or to-and-fro movement.

rotary motion A rotating, spinning or turning movement.

satellite A device put into orbit around a planet, moon or other object in space.

simple machine A basic machine that does one simple job, such as a lever.

steam Hot water vapour that forms when water turns from a liquid into a gas.

turbine A device that converts a flow of a fluid, such as water, steam or air, into a rotary motion that can be used to power machines or generate electricity.

vacuum A space that has nothing in it at all, not even air.

FURTHER INFORMATION

WEBSITES

Exploratorium Science Snacks: Engineering and Technology
www.exploratorium.edu/snacks/subject/engineering-and-technology

ScienceKids: Engineering for Kids
www.sciencekids.co.nz/engineering.html

NeoK12 Simple Machines
www.neok12.com/Simple-Machines.htm

Animated Engines
www.animatedengines.com

Science Trek: Simple Machines
idahoptv.org/sciencetrek/topics/simple_machines/facts.cfm

WEBSITES ABOUT MAKING

Tate Kids: Make
www.tate.org.uk/kids/make

PBS Design Squad Global
pbskids.org/designsquad

Instructables
www.instructables.com

Make:
makezine.com

WHERE TO BUY MATERIALS

Hobbycraft
For art and craft materials
www.hobbycraft.co.uk

B&Q
For pipes, tubing, wood, glue and other hardware
www.diy.com

Fred Aldous
For art and craft materials, photography supplies and books
www.fredaldous.co.uk

BOOKS

Awesome Engineering series by Sally Spray (Franklin Watts, 2017)

Cause, Effect and Chaos!: In Engineering and Industry by Paul Mason (Wayland, 2018)

How Machines Work by David Macualay (Dorling Kindersley, 2015)

Home Lab by Robert Winston and Jack Challoner (Dorling Kindersley, 2016)

Machines and Motors: Infographic How it Works by Jon Richards and Ed Simkins (Wayland, 2016)

PLACES TO VISIT

Science Museum, London, UK
www.sciencemuseum.org.uk

Museum of Science and Industry, Manchester, UK
www.msimanchester.org.uk

MAD (Mechanical Art and Design) Museum, Stratford-Upon-Avon, UK
themadmuseum.co.uk

INDEX